Titletown U.S.A.

Tailgaten Cookbook

6th Edition

A Publication Of
Tailgaten Cookbooks
Ixonia, Wisconsin

TITLETOWN U.S.A.
Tailgaten Cookbook

Sixth Edition 2001
Copyright 2001 Donald D. Sabatke

Published by: Donald D. Sabatke
N8443 Swansea Drive
Ixonia, Wisconsin 53036

> This book is a collection of favorite recipes,
> which are not necessarily original recipes
> but were provided by the Tailgaters
> listed in this book.

Publisher, Editor and Designer:
Donald D. Sabatke

Master Photographer
David Vanderkin

Assistant Photographers
Nancy Vanderkin-Doris Sabatke

ISBN: 0-9659071-5-5
Library of Congress Catalog Card Number: 01-12698

> All photos, information and recipes in this book are being used with the
> permission of those that appear in the publication. Opinions expressed
> in this publication are not necessarily endorsed, nor does the publication
> assume responsibility for statements made.

No part of this publication may be reproduced
or copied in any form or by an means without
written permission of the publishers.

Printed In The United States

Tailgaten Cookbook   6th Edition

Tailgaten

Year after year the Packer fans return to lambeau for the fun of Tailgaten. The fantastic food, the refreshing drinks and the good cheer of seeing old friends is what tailgaten is all about. This year was a little different because of the renovation of Lambeau field. Parking places were cut and lines to enter Lambeau were long, but it was all worth it to see the Packers in action. This year marked the 6th year for the staff of the Tailgaten Cookbook to take pictures in the parking lot for the publication. The weather was a big factor this year as we had rain on several days but still the fans came. The 6th edition is a special edition because it has some great shots of the stadium as it gets a face lift. The addition is going up fast and should be really great when finished. The Tailgaters were great this year. They come from all over Wisconsin and several surrounding states and always cook the greatest food. From lobster to hot dogs, chili to T-bones, you will see it all at the Tailgaten parties before every home game. If you haven't tried Tailgaten, you are missing the action. Next year get in line, enter Lambeau field 4 hours before game time, start your grill and enjoy the fine sport of Tailgaten. Throw some extra coals on the fire and smile, you could be in the 7th edition of the Tailgaten Cookbook.

Join The Fun.........
Tailgaten At
Lambeau!

Contents

The cities represented in this publication are listed in alphabetical order.

Cities   *Page Numbers*

Algoma--68
Antigo---43
Appleton--27-35-65-70-73-75-83
Ashwaubenon---28
Beloit---45-65-78
Berlin---46
Bessemer, MI--19
Brodhead--47
Brookfield---42-52
Brooklyn Center---19
Brown Deer--61
Burlington---16-33-54-55-60
Butler---51
Cedarburg---35-48
Crivitz---33
DeForest---18
Denmark---21
DePere--29-37-38-66
Edgerton---62
Elkhorn--54
Fennimore---59
Fond du Lac--14-32-42-71
Green Bay-12-17-22-23-25-26-27-28-30-38-39-53-63-67-68-69-71-73-77-79-81
Hartland---44-50
Janesville--15
Jefferson--45
Kaukauna--24-72-80
Kenosha---50

Cities   *Page Numbers*

Keshena	36
Lakewood	13
Luxemburg	26
Madison	43
Manitowoc	37-40
Maple Grove	36
Mayville	16
Menasha	21-24-58
Menomonee Falls	4-53
Merrill	79
Middleton	55
Milwaukee	46-48-59
Minneapolis, MN	74
Mishawaka, IN	58
Mountain	34
Neenah	21-64-74
North Fond du Lac	14
Oconomowoc	31
Onalaska	52
Oshkosh	76
Park Ridge, IL	52
Pickerel	11
Plymouth	18
Pulaski	34
Racine	12-60
Ringle	76
Rolling Meadow, IL	32
Seymour	31-70
Shawano	11
Sheboygan	29-44
Sioux Falls, SD	15-80
Sobieski	69-77
Stevens Point	49-66-78
Stow, OH	20

Cities   *Page Numbers*

Sturgeon Bay--39
Tomahawk---20
Watertown---56
Wausau---20-67
West Allis--40-57
Whitefish Bay---42
Whitewater--57
Winona, MN--43
Woodville---49

Other Pages In This Edition

Cover page--1
Title Page---2
Tailgaten--3
Contents--4-5-6
Lambeau Renovation---7-8-9
Pack Rats---82
Aprons--84
Tailgaten Cookbook Back Editions---85
The Great Recipe Hunt---86
Disclaimer--87
Tailgaten Cookbook Order Form--89

Coming Soon!

The greatest Tailgaten Cookbook ever!
All the recipes from the past 5 editions of the Tailgaten Cookbook
in one book. No tailgaten pictures, just recipes.
Hundreds and hundreds of them.
<u>Sorted in Main dishes, Deserts, Snacks</u>
If you would like us to notify you when this book comes out, send us your
name and address at Tailgaten Cookbook, N8443 Swansea Drive, Ixonia 53036
or Email us at:

dsabatke@nconnect.net

Lambeau.. The Renovation

Tailgaten Cookbook   **6th Edition**

| Tailgaten Cookbook   6th Edition | 9 |

Tailgaten Cookbook   6th Edition

Light The Grills

Set The Table

Lets Party!

Tailgaten Cookbook   6th Edition   11

Pickerel

Left to right: Sandy Falk, Bobbi Braun, Mary Lou Paulson, Lisa Volkman

Antigo Girls "Captain Concoction"

1 bottle of Captain Morgan spiced rum, 64 oz. orange juice, 64 oz. cranberry juice cocktail. Mix in 2 gal. pitcher. Serve over ice.

Shawano

Stephanie Glaser, Pat Glaser, Tim Carew

—Vegetable Pizza—

2 pkgs crescent rolls
2 (8 oz) pkg. cream cheese
2/3 cup mayonnaise
1/4 tsp onion powder or 1 tsp onion flakes
1/2 pkg Hidden Valley ranch dressing (dry)
Broccoli, cauliflower, carrots, black olives, shredded cheese.

Directions

Press 2 packages crescent roll dough out on large pizza pan or jelly roll pan. Pinch together perforations. Bake according to directions on package. Let cool. Beat together the remaining ingredients. Spread over baked and cooled crust. Cover with the following finely chopped vegetables:
Broccoli, cauliflower, carrots, black olives. Sprinkle with finely shredded cheese.

Green Bay

Left to right: George Rohe, Marlene Rohe, George Mason, Jeff Morris, Kathy Clark, Mike Kryszak, Vicky VandenAvond, Pam Morris, Leroy VandenAvond

Racine

Left to right: Dana Thielen, Dan Thielen, Joel Adamczyk, Richele Adamczyk

First Down Slush

1 can of frozen lemonade
1 can frozen orange juice
7 cups of water, 2 cups of brandy
Mix above all together
2 cups boiling water
2 cups sugar
4 tsp ice tea mix (for color)
Mix together, then mix with above and freeze for 48 hours. Serve with 7-up. Makes 1 gallon

Tailgaten Cookbook   6th Edition

Lakewood

Left to right: Tom Wurzer, Rita Griffiths, Crys Petersen, Terry Rank, Sandy Lettenberger, Pete Rank, Dave Seeber, Kathy Rank, Kim Tucker Seeber, Erin Rank Seeber, Ralph Petersen, Bob Seeber, Randy Jackett, Denise Jackett.

Drunken Rib-Eye Sandwiches

Cut rib-eye steaks thin (3/8 inch)
Marinate overnite in Jim Beam steak sauce
Grill to liking. Serve on your favorite kind of roll.
*The Jim Beam in the steak sauce evaporates during grilling so any age can enjoy!
(Great on chicken breasts too)

Fond du Lac

Don Miller & Sally Auchtung

Taco Salad

1 lb hamburger
brown, drain and cool
1 head lettuce
tear into pieces
2 diced tomatoes
1 can kidney beans
1 pkg shredded cheese (1 lb.)
1 large bag taco flavored Doritoes crushed
1 qt. bottle of catalina or Western salad dressing
Combine together all ingredients, pour dressing over and mix.
May not be entire bottle of dressing.

North Fond du Lac

Cherilyn Yapp, Richard Yapp, Paul Stephany, Judy Stephany, Pat Crowley, Carol Crowley, Kathy & Patrick

Layered Shrimp Dip

1 pkg. 3 oz. cream cheese
6 tbsp salsa (divided)
1/2 cup cocktail sauce
3 cans (6 oz. each) small shrimp
rinsed & drained or 1 lb bag frozen small shrimp

1 cup shredded cheddar cheese
1 cup shredded monterey jack cheese
sliced green onions
diced tomatoe
1 can (2-1/4 oz(sliced ripe olives (drained)

Combine cream cheese and 3 tbsp salsa - spread into ungreased glass 9" pie plate. Combine cocktail sauce and remaining salsa. Spread over cream cheese. Place shrimp evenly over top. Sprinkle with olives. Combine cheeses. Sprinkle over olives. Top with onions and tomatoes. Chill and serve with tortilla chips.

Tailgaten Cookbook 6th Edition 15

Janesville

Donna Wegner & Carolyn Kroes

Green Bay Packer Cake

2 oz. green food coloring
3 tbsp sweet milk cocoa (Nestle's Quick)
1/2 cup butter flavor crisco
2 eggs, beaten
1 cup buttermilk
1 tsp soda
1 tsp salt
1 tbsp vinegar
1 tsp vanilla
2 1/2 cup cake flour

Cream the Crisco, sugar and eggs. Make paste of the food coloring and Nestle's milk cocoa. Add to beaten egg mixture. Add buttermilk with salt and vanilla. Alternate with the flour. Mix and remove from the electric mixer. Fold in the vinegar and baking soda. Bake in two 9 inch well greased and floured layer cake pans at 350 degrees for 30 to 35 minutes. Let cool in cake pans for 5 minutes.

Carolyn Kroes, Janesville

Buttercream Frosting

1/2 cup solid vegetable shortening - 1/2 cup butter or margarine - 1 tsp vanilla
5 cups powdered sugar - 3 tbsp milk - Yellow Food coloring

In a large bowl, cream butter and shortening with electric mixer. Add vanilla. Gradually add sugar, one cup at a time, beating well on medium speed. Scrape sides and bottom of bowl often. When you reach the third cup of powdered sugar, add 1 tablespoon of milk to moisten. Continue the same with the fourth and fifth cup of powdered sugar. Add the yellow food coloring to desired shade.

Donna Wegner, Kaukauna

Packer Superbowl Pizza

1 tube croissants
Bacon - onion - pepperoni - lettuce
1/2 cup mayo - 3 tsp mustard

Arrange croissants on a pizza pan so as to create a pizza crust. Cook as directed. When cool apply mustard/mayo mixture to taste. Apply lettuce, bacon, onion, pepporoni as desired. Refrigerate 1 hour and enjoy.

Sioux Falls, SD

Left to right, Cole Meunier, Scott Meunier, Kathy Meunier, Michelle Leopold

Burlington

Packer Party Peanut Butter Treats

1/4 cup margarine
1 package (10 oz) mini marshmallows
3/4 cup creamy peanut butter
5 cups Rice Krispies
1 cup (6 oz) butterscotch chips
1 cup (6 oz) semisweet chocolate chips

In a large saucepan melt butter and marshmallows. Remove from heat, stir in peanut butter. Gradually add cereal, mix until well coated. Spread and press into a greased 13x9x2 pan, set aside. In double boiler melt the chips. Spread over cereal mixture. Cover and freeze for 15-20 minutes or until chocolate is set.

Christine Cooper, Burlington

Paul Cooper, Christine Cooper,
Bridget Krupp, Dave Krupp

Packer Party Potatoes

2 lb. package frozen hash browns (southern style - 1 stick margarine
2 cups shredded mild cheddar cheese - 1/2 cup chopped onion - 1 can cream of chicken soup
2 cups sour cream (16 oz) - 1 tsp salt - 1 tsp pepper - 2/3 cups corn flakes

Mix all above ingredients together except the corn flakes. Place in 13x9x2 baking dish and top with corn flakes. Bake at 350 degrees for 1 hour.

Bridget Krupp, Burlington

Mayville

Larry & Nancy La Charite

Tailgaten Cookbooks Make Great Gifts

—

Order Today

Green Bay

Left to right, Joe Schermetzler, Adam Koch, Brian Koch, Deb Koch, Sandie Koch, Leroy Koch. In front row, Bobby Koch.

Koch Booyah

2 chickens cooked and deboned
2 lbs carrots, diced
5 lbs potatoes peeled and diced
1 medium head cabbage cored and chopped
2 lbs chopped celery - 2 lbs diced onions
1 lb can diced tomatoes - 1 can tomato juice
1 lb beef stew meat or 3 beef soup bones
(more flavor with soup bones)
Cook until tender. Serve hot with a lot of crackers. Its best for the December games!!!!!
Sandie Koch, Brillion

Packer Omelets

1 dozen eggs - 1 lb diced boiled ham
8 oz package shredded sharp cheddar cheese
1 green pepper diced
2 medium diced onions
1 can 8oz sliced mushrooms
1 stick butter.
Melt margarine or butter. Scramble eggs and add 1/2 cup water or milk. Have one BIG skillet. Add eggs and other ingredients. Cook until eggs are set. Serve with muffins.
Serves 6
Deb Koch, Green Bay

Beef Philly Sandwiches

4 lbs Ribeye steak (sliced thin)
1 green pepper sliced
1 sliced onion
1 lb sliced mushrooms
1 stick butter or margarine
Saute in Foil all of above
Grill steak for desired doneness. Have green pepper, onion and mushrooms handy in foil to serve over steak on french bread or hard roll.
Bobby Koch, Manitowoc

De Forest

Joel Capaul, Tim Esser, Tonya Choice, Dennis Simpson

Philly Free Cheesehead Cake

3 packages (8 oz each) Philly free creamcheese (softened)
3/4 cup sugar - 1 tsp vanilla - 3 eggs (to reduce fat use eggbeaters)
1/3 cup lowfat graham cracker crumbs (I use low fat cinnamon grahams)
1 1/2 cup strawberry slices or any fruit
Mix cream cheese , sugar and vanilla (mix well) Add eggs. Mix just until blended.
DO NOT overbeat after adding eggs. Spray 9 inch pie plate with no stick cooking spray. Sprinkle bottom with graham cracker crumbs. Pour cream cheese mixture into prepared pie plate. Bake at 325 for 45 minutes or until center is almost set. Refrigerate 3 hours or overnight. Top with fruit.

Tonya Choice, Madison

Plymouth

Gene Blindauer & Jenny Blindauer

BBQ Chicken

Seasonings for 30 chickens
(left over seasoning will keep a long time when stored in an airtight container.

26 oz salt
8 oz pepper
8 oz paprika

cut chicken in halve, sprinkle skin area with seasoning. lay on grill, seasoned side up. Do not turn chicken. Leave on grill 1 hour.

Tailgaten Cookbook   6th Edition   19

Brooklyn Center

Harry Maass, Scott Wickland, Marlene Cooley, Rox Maass

Hot Chocolate With A Kick

6 oz hot chocolate - 1 1/2 oz Jack Daniel's
1/2 oz almond or coffee liqueur
Stir Jack Daniel's and Liqueur into mug of hot chocolate. Garnish with a marshmallow.

BLT Dip

1/2 bottle Hellman's mayo
16 oz sour cream - 1 cup real bacon bits
4 small tomatoes, cut fine
Mix ingredients. Serve with crackers, chips or bread cubes.
Jonelle M. France, Bessemer

Harry's Ribs

2 racks baby back pork ribs
1-2 liter bottle of Coca-Cola
Simmer ribs for 1 hour in Coca-Cola. Season with your favorite dry rub (garlic powder, pepper or whatever you wish) Refrigerate until ready to use.
Grill over hot coals until browned (30 minutes), brush with BBQ sauce last 10 minutes. Serve 1/2 rack per person. These are great and people will think you cooked them over the grill all day!
Harry Maass, South Milwaukee

Bessemer, Michigan

Bernie Michelli & Jonelle M. France

The Tailgaten Cookbook... What Packer Fans Eat...... Give A Book To A Friend!

Tomahawk

Left to right, Nicole Walters, Shirley Ament, Ron Ament, Eric Smith

Roast Beef "Venison" Barbecue

4 tbsp A-1 sauce
2 tbsp Worcestershire sauce
2 tbsp brown sugar
2 tbsp salad oil
1 can tomato soup (no water)
Bring to a boil and simmer a little bit and put over meat. Makes about 3 lb. Use with ham, beef, venison or anything. You can just brown the venison and put everything into a crock pot and let it cook all day. Real Good!!!!!

Ron Ament, Tomahawk

Grilled Salmon

(for 1-2 lb filet)
1/2 cup soy sauce
1/4 cup lemon, lime or orange juice
3 tbsp olive oil
1 1/2 tsp crushed garlic
1 1/2 tsp basil
Mix all ingredients and marrinate filet for 2-24 hours. Place on foil on grill and cover. Cook until firm.

Mike McGinnity, Wausau

Wausau

Jim McGinnity, Greg Fochs, Mike McGinnity, Tom Leahy, Allen Paul, Brandon Bean

Stow, Ohio

Jeff Brummel, Dana Morales, Kelly Smith, Mike Davis

Juicy Brats

In a large pot of water add 3 or 4 beef boullion cubes, 2 medium onions sliced and seperated into rings. Add brats. Simmer 4 or 5 hours on a very low heat. Grill till golden brown. They will stay plump and juicy even when re-heated.

Dana Morales, Stow, Ohio

Tailgaten Cookbook   6th Edition   21

Menasha

Peggy & Carl Kennedy

Neenah

Bill Devine, Ginny Devine,
Mary Hooper, Foss Hooper

Grilled Chicken Breast Sandwiches

Marinate chicken breasts in italian dressing and grill. Also grill fresh Hungarian chilies (mild) or whole mild canned chilies. When chicken breasts are almost done, top with a slice of jack cheese. Serve chicken breasts and chilies on buns with mayonnaise,
Mary Hooper, Neenah

Mandarin Orange Torte

60 Ritz crackers, crushed
1/2 cup butter, melted - 1/2 cup sugar
1 cup sweetened condensed milk
1 - 13 oz container Cool Whip topping
1 - 6 oz can frozen orange juice
(concentrated and thawed)
3 - 11 oz cans mandarin oranges, drained

Mix crackers with butter and sugar. Press into a 9 x 13 inch baking pan, reserving 1/2 cup of crumbs for topping. Blend sweetened condensed milk and cool whip and orange juice concentrate. Fold in mandarin oranges and pour mixture over crust, top with remaining crumbs. Freeze until 15 minutes before serving.
Serives 12-15
Peggy Kennedy, Menasha

Denmark

Shirley Paider, Bill Paider,
Ritchie Stitch, Tina Stitch

Order An Extra Copy Of The Tailgaten Cookbook For Your Packer Friends!

Green Bay
"The Packalope"

Front Row, Julie Weslin, Denver, Co., Rochelle Dreiling, Denver, Co., Second Row, Bombo Alexa, Iron River, MI, Fred Bronge & June Bronge, Lake Zurich, IL, Scott Weslen, Denver, Co, Sue "Mrs Lope" Primeau, Ann Durst, DeForest, Marcia Toretti, Iron Mountain, MI, Third Row, a Friend, Jamie Cahill, Appleton, Heidi, Brian "Green and Gold Elvis" Wedin, Appleton, Conni Wedin, Appleton, Dave Johnson, Stevens Point, a Friend, Larry "Packalope" Primeau, Elgie Suplicki, Stevens Point, Denny Durst, DeForest, Bill Doxrude, Stevens Point, Bruce Toreth, Iron Mountain, MI, Kevin Ruder, Stevens Point, Stan Potacki, Stevens Point.

Great Food Ideas From Larry and Sue Primeau (Mr, & Mrs, Packalope)

Jack's Cheese Head Tailgating Spread

2 cups shredded Wisconsin sharp cheddar cheese - 1 package (8 oz softened cream cheese
1 tbsp Dijon mustard - 2 tbsp chopped green onions
2 tbsp Jack Daniels Old #7 - Dash hot pepper sauce.
Mix ingredients together. Place in serving dish. Chill and serve with crackers or favorite veggies.

The Lope's Zucchini Munchies

3 cup sliced thin zucchini - 1 cup bisquick
1/2 cup green chopped onions
1/2 cup grated Parmesan cheese
2 tbsp chopped parsley
1/2 tsp each of pepper, salt, italian seasoning
1/4 tsp garlic powder - dash of Tabasco sauce
1/2 cup oil - 4 beaten eggs
Mix all ingredients together and spread in a greased and floured 9 x 13 glass baking dish. Bake at 350 for 25 to 30 minutes. Cool and cut into squares. Serve hot or cold.

BBQ Bacon Wrapped Grilled Shrimp and Scallops

1 lb (16-20 count) shrimp, peeled and deveined
10-20 count fresh sea scallops
6-8 strips thick cut bacon - BBQ sauce of choice
Cut each slice of bacon in 3 pieces. Place shrimp on bacon and roll bacon around shrimp. Use toothpicks to hold together. Do the same with the scallops. Place on grill and cook till bacon is crispy. Remove from grill and dip in sauce to cover. Return to grill and finish cooking 1 more minute.

Taffy Apple Salad

1 (20 oz) can crushed pineapple drained - save juice
2 cups mini marshmallows
1/2 cup sugar - 1 tbsp flour - 1 beaten egg
1 tsp vinegar - 1 (12 oz) cool whip - 2 cups peeled and diced apples
1 1/2 cup cocktail or spanish peanuts

Mix pineapple and marshmallows and refrigerate overnight. Combine pineapple juice, flour, sugar, vinegar and egg. Cook over medium heat stirring constantly (use wire whisk). Place in fridge overnight. The next day mix cool whip and both mixtures together. Stir in nuts and apples. Reserve some nuts to sprinkle on top. Chill 2 more hours and enjoy.

Kaukauna

Margie & Dan Verbeten

The Tailgaten Cookbook A Great Gift Idea!

Seasoned Oyster Crackers

3/4 cup vegetable oil - 2 tbsp dill weed
1 pkg dry ranch dressing mix
1 pkg oyster crackers

Mix oil, dill weed and ranch dressing. Place oyster crackers in brown paper bag. Pour liquid mixture in bag, close top and shake to coat crackers. Spread crackers on cookie sheet and bake in warm oven for 15 minutes.

Snack In A Bag

1 stick butter - 1/2 cup corn syrup
1 cup brown sugar - 8 oz pretzels
1 box Crispix cereal - 2 cups peanuts
1 lb M & M's - 1 tsp vanilla
1 tsp baking soda

Combine butter, corn syrup, sugar and baking soda. Microwave for 2 minutes on high. Stir and microwave 2 more minutes. Add vanilla and baking soda and stir. Pour Crispix cereal in a brown paper bag, add the mix over the top and mix with a spoon. Microwave 1 1/2 minutes, shake bag and repeat once. Add pretzels and nuts and shake. Cool and add M & M's.

Margie Verbeten, Kaukauna

"Our Favorite" Spanish Hamburger

Fry 2 lbs ground meat and 1 chopped onion. Add 2 tbsp vinegar, 2 tbsp brown sugar, 4 tbsp lemon juice, 3 tbsp worchestershire sauce, 1/2 tsp mustard (ground double fine), 1 cup catsup, 1/2 cup water, salt and pepper to taste. Simmer 1/2 hour or longer. Serves 12

Luann M. Streur, Menasha

Heather M. Streur, Luann M. Streur, Christine Kellner, Nicole Ak. Streur

Tailgaten Cookbook   6th Edition   25

Green Bay

Front Row: Alta Sloan, Rich Sloan, Donna Colbert. Back Row: Frank Newell, Cindy Newell, Mike Colbert

Grilled Shrimp Scampi Kabobs

2 lbs fresh tiger shrimp (large) 1 cup olive oil - 8 tbsp butter
4 fresh garlic - minced fresh veggies including cherry tomatoes, green peppers, mushrooms, green onions, red peppers. Warm oil and butter and add garlic and steam for 15 minutes. Marinate shrimp 20-30 minutes. Thread skewers and grill until shrimp are pink.

Green Bay

Front Row: Ryan, Dawn & Gloria. Back Row: Tira, Donna, Patti, Kevin, Rich, P.J., Dave, Darrell, Joe.

Green Bay

Left to Right: Erin Hibbard, Jesse DeByl, Sherry Anderson, Mary Krueser, Andy Ebert, Dave Krueser, Jenny Krueser

Luxemburg

Back Row: Bob Barnum, Barb Maenpaa, Jason Barnum
Front Row:, Friend, Friend, Friend, Andrea Barnum

Chicken & Okra Gumbo

2 1/2 to 3 lb chicken boiled and cut-up - 2 qts water - 1/4 cup oil
2 tbsp flour - 2 medium chopped onions - 1 cup celery chopped - 3 garlic cloves minced
1 can 28 oz tomatoes drained - 2 cup fresh or frozen okra pieces - 2 bay leaves - 1 tsp salt
1 tsp basil - 1/2 tsp pepper - 2 to 3 tsp Tabasco.

Cook chicken reserve broth. In separate pan cook oil and flour until smooth, cook about 5 minutes until reddish brown. Add 2 cups chicken broth and cook until thick, add vegetables and spices and simmer on low for 2 hours. Serve with rice or add rice to gumbo. 8-10 servings.

Green Bay

Roy Miller, Pete Baeten, Sue Leet, Chris Brooks, Jamie Kihell, Lori Miller, Carrie Baeten

Grandma's Chip Dip

2 packages cream cheese - 1/2 tsp celery salt - 1/4 tsp garlic powder - 1 small diced onion
4-5 tbsp milk or cream
Blend all ingredients to desired consistency, add more liquid if needed.

Sue Leet, Sheboygan Falls

Appleton

Front Row: Melanie "Yo Nellie" De Karske, Cary "Loco Weed" Welch. Back Row. Pat "Pugger" Groves, Ken "Kenny" McClelland, Don "Shwanky" Springhetti, Ray "Harv" Harvey, Dennis "Big Den" Groves, Bil "Billibob" Hastie, Lisa "Looper" Harvey, Greg "Hinks" Hinkens

Barry's Finger Lickin Hotwings

Cut chicken wings at joint into two pieces, season with cayenne pepper and salt and cook on grill. Simmer in kettle 1 bottle Louisiana hotsauce, worstershire and butter. Shake fully cooked wing pieces in simmering sauce and serve with blue cheese dressing and celery stalks.

Green Bay

Notre Dame Chili

2- 1 lb cans kidney beans
3 large onions chopped
3 green peppers chopped
2 1/2 lb ground beef
1 - 1 lb can tomatoes diced
3 - 15 oz cans tomato sauce
3-4 tbsp chili powder
1/4 tsp cumin
1/4 tsp cayenne pepper
2 tsp salt.

Brown onions, green pepper and meat. Drain fat. Add beans and rest of ingredients. Cover and simmer 1 1/2 to 2 hours. Serve with grated cheese if you wish. Serves a large number of Packer fans.

Jane Phelps, Green Bay

Front Row: Susan Phelps, Jane Glyzewski. Back Row: Jane Phelps, Becky Glyzewski, Bernie Phelps, Jerry Meyer, Dave Glyzewski, Karen Smudde, Ed Chaltry.

Ashwaubenon

Ron and Pat Steers

Secret Sause

1 pkg Hidden Valley ranch mix for buttermilk
1/2 cup buttermilk
2 cups Hellmans mayo
1/2 jar Pace picante HOT (16 oz)

Disolve ranch mix in 1/2 cup buttermilk, to this add and mix in 2 cups mayo, add 1/2 jar of picante. This is good as a dip or as a sauce for anything. We like it on our quarter back crunches. That recipe next year.

Pat Steers, Ashwaubenon

Get All 5 Back Issues Of the Tailgaten Cookbook A Real Collectors Item

Tailgaten Cookbook   6th Edition   29

De Pere

Front Row: Mike Way, Paul Micksch. Back Row: Buzz Owens, Jeremy Smith, Brain Tomchech, Brad Tomchech, Jason Derpinghaus

Sheboygan

Jerry Cook, Sharon Cook, Becky Hayes, Jerry Hayes

Green Bay

Front Row: Dave Jantz, Larry Ball, Francis Kidd, Nicole Geniesse, Mike Geniesse
Back Row: Chris Kidd, Kim Schaefer, Beau Andrew, Andrew Geniesse

Chicken Wings

10 lbs chicken wings frozen - 1 bottle wing sauce - 1 habenero pepper
Deep fry wings in oil at 375 until they float. Flip in wing sauce and crushed habenero pepper. Place in crock pot on low till game time. Eat and enjoy.

Francis Kidd, Pembine

Green Bay

Front Row: Mike Wartel, Crystal Volyan, Friend. Middle Row: Cristy Posslay, Scott Schwartz, Lisa Evans, Friend, Friend. Back Row: Friend, Dan Ockar, Friend, Ben Dastaercke, Jill Nooyan

Tenderloin Tips

2 tbsp pepper oil - 2 lb beef tendeloin tips, cut thin - 2 tbsp butter - 2 tsp salt 1 cup sliced mushrooms - 1/4 cup chopped onions - 1 clove garlic, minced - 1/2 cup burgandy wine - 1/2 cup J.D. whiskey - 1 cup crushed tomatoes - 2 beef bouillon cubes - 2 tsp sugar.

Saute meat quick in butter and pepper oil until browned. Add salt, mushrooms, onion and garlic. Simmer until onions carmalize. Add wine, whiskey, tomatoes, bouillion and sugar. Simmer for 30 minutes or until tender.

Scott Schwartz, Green Bay

Tailgaten Cookbook   6th Edition   31

Oconomowoc

George Washington Chili

2 lb ground chuck
1 lb lean pork
2 chopped onions
2 minced garlic cloves
2 packages chili seasoning mix
1 - 28 oz can whole tomatoes
1 - 6 oz can tomato paste
1 - 1 lb can refried beans
Salt

Brown beef, pork, onions, garlic. Pour off fat. Add seasoning mix and 2 cups water, tomatoes and paste, beans and salt. Simmer and serve.

Chris Dambeck, Oconomowoc

Larry Dambeck, Chris Dambeck, Phil Brown, Mike Dambeck

Seymour

Front Row: Pat Kuhar, Candy Wilke, Kim Marnocha
Back Row: Joe Kuhar, Dale Wilke, Greg Marnocha

Cheese Pototoes

2 lb bag frozen hashbrowns - 1 tsp garlic salt - 1 med. onion, chopped - 1 1/2 stick margarine melted (set aside 1/2 stick for topping) - 1 8oz pkg shredded cheddar cheese - 1 pt sour cream 2 cans cream of chicken soup - 2 cups corn flakes.

Mix together all ingredients, except for 1/2 stick margarine and cornflakes. Put in 9 x 13 pan. Melt remaining 1/2 stick margarine and add 2 cups crushed cornflakes and mix together. Place on top of potatoes and bake at 350 for 1 hour.

Kim Marnocha, Seymour

Rolling Meadow, IL

Pizza On The Grill

Pizza Crust
1 cup tomato sauce
1 cup sliced mushrooms
1 cup sliced sausage (Italian)
onion and peppers to taste
1/2 can sliced olives
1 bag mozzarella cheese
Shredded. Put directly on hot grill. Pile high with ingredients. Cover and cook 25-30 minutes or until crust is brown on bottom. Crust can be purchased at local store. We purchase all out meat from the the deli in Chicago. Slice and enjoy.
Liz Pegorsch, Rolling Meadow

Front: Liz Pegorsch, Allison Pegorsch
Back: Zachary Pegorsch, Michael Pegorsch

Ham Rollups

8 oz reduced fat cream cheese softened
1-2 tbsp sour cream reduced fat
1/4 tsp onion powder
1/8 tsp garlic powder
6-8 lg. thin slices deli ham
12-16 baby dill pickles drained
Blend cream cheese, sour cream, onion and garlic powder until smooth and creamy. With back of spoon, evenly spread cheese mixture on slice of ham. Place pickle onto ham and carefully roll up. Place toothpicks into ham and pickle to secure. Cut into 3/4 inch pieces. You can also use smoked turkey breast in place of ham and add 1/2 tsp of dry mustard to the cheese mixture.
Lori Cardinal, Fond du Lac

Fond du Lac

Jack Brayton, Mary Brayton, Lori Cardinal, Jim Cardinal

Burlington

Sharon Angelici, David Angelici, Phil De Greef, Marilyn De Greef

Bratwurst Relish

Onion - Green Pepper
Tomato

Chop all of the above very fine.
Use amount to your liking.
Add salt and pepper
and garlic salt and you are ready
to go.
This is almost too easy.
Some like more tomato, some
more onion.
Top that brat and enjoy.
Marilyn De Greef, Burlington

Crivitz

Melissa Bolling, Bonnie Vann, Kim Hanson, David Queoff, Tom Queoff, Kevin Hanson

Pulaski

James Meyers, Stephanie Meyers, Mike Johnson, Kim Johnson, Gregory Meyers, Lindsey Peterson

Carmel Corn

5 quarts popped popcorn (2 batches in air popper) - 2 sticks butter - 2 cups brown sugar
1/2 cup white corn syrup - pinch of salt - pinch of cream of tartar
Combine and boil 5 minutes. Remove from heat and add 1 tsp baking soda and stir.
Put popcorn in large roaster pan and pour caramel over top and stir until coated well.
Bake for 1 hour at 200. Stir every 5 minutes.

Kim Johnson, Pulaski

Mountain

Crab Dip

1 stick butter
1 lb Velveta cheese
1 can crab (minced)
Heat and serve with Triscuits.
**Laurie Kinziger
Mountain**

Laurie Kinziger, Mary Pashouwer, Jeff Kinziger, Kristal Kinziger, Jeanne Kabat, Terry Kabat

Cedarburg

Karla Marsolek & Brian Kluever

Baked Beans

1 - 16 oz can pork & beans or baked beans
1 - 16 oz can butter beans
1 - 16 oz can kidney beans
1/2 lb hamburger
1/4 lb bacon
1 onion - 1/4 cup ketchup
1/2 cup brown sugar
1/4 cup sugar - 1 tbsp molasses
Brown hamburger & drain. Chop onion and brown with drained hamburger. Cook bacon, drain & crumble into bits. Combine all ingredients in baking pan or Nesco and bake or cook at 350 for 1 hour or until desired consistency.
Karla Marsolek, Cedarburg

Appleton

John Ray, Mark Snyder, Dave Drier, Sherry Ray, Dan Drier, Cori Snyder

Venison Chili

3 lbs cubed venison steak - 15 oz can dark beans - 15 oz can lite beans - 2 - 15 oz cans stewed tomatoes, large red onion chopped, 2 jalapenos chopped - 2 tbsp chopped garlic large can tomatoes - 4-12 oz cans of beer - 3 pkgs chili mix - 1 green, yellow and red pepper chopped. Brown meat and drain, add the rest of ingredients and 3 cans of beer. (drink one) Serve over Fritos with shredded cheese and onion on top.
Sherry Ray, Appleton

Keshena

Beverly Muehlius, Jessia Balster,
Heather Lee Muehlius, Dean Muehlius

" The Muehlius Party Tray"

Maple Grove

Angelo Papademetriou, Alexandra Papademetriou, Debbie Papademetriou, Amy Frisque, Lon Frisque, Nancy Frisque, Steve Relton

Lambeau Field Bean Dip

1 can of Hormel Hot with beans chili - 1 can of Hormel Hot with no beans chili
1 can Hormel regular with beans chili - 1 can Hormel regular with no beans chili
1 can Hormel Tabasco Sauce with beans chili - 2 pkg 8 oz cream cheese - 2-3 pounds of shredded cheese
Scoop Fritos or quesadilla chips. Add cream cheese to chili and heat in sauce pan at medium temp. Add shredded cheese last and heat until melted. Put in pot or old coffee can that can be heated on a grill at the game. Make sure you bring a wooden spoon that can be used to stir the dip while it is heating.

Tailgaten Cookbook   6th Edition   37

De Pere

All Purpose Dry Rub

1/4 cup kosher salt
1/2 cup brown sugar
1/2 cup hungarian paprika
tbsp ground black pepper
2 tbsp chili powder
2 tsp dry mustard
1/2 tsp cayenne
1 tsp ground cumin

Blend together and store in a cool dry place. Rub generously into roasts, ribs or any meat pieces. Store in Ziplock bag, preferably overnight, until ready to grill or roast.

Larry A. Busse, De Pere

Larry T. Busse, Heather Kandrat, Caryl Busse, Larry A. Busse

Manitowoc

Mary Jo & John (Jack) Kocourek

Mary Jo's Gramma Cookies - Original Recipe!

2 sticks margarine - 1 cup peanut butter
3/4 cup brown sugar - 1/2 cup white sugar
2 eggs - 1 tsp vanilla

1 cup flour - 1 cup whole wheat flour
1 1/2 cup oatmeal - 1 tsp baking soda
1/2 tsp salt - 2 cups chocolate chips

Cream maragarine & peanut butter together. Add sugars, beat till fluffy. Add eggs, beat, add vanilla, beat. Slowly add dry ingredients. Mix in Chocolate chips. Scoop onto cookie sheets with cookie scoop or teaspoon. Flatten with fork. Bake at 350 for 10-12 minutes. Nuts are optional

Tailgaten Cookbook 6th Edition

Green Bay

Jeff Kleiner, Shannon Kleiner, Rich Sloan, Alta Sloan, Debra Ward, Corey Schroeder

Guacamole Packer Style

3 soft avocadoes lightly mashed - 3 garlic cloves minced
2 tbsp cilantro - 1/4 tsp fresh lime juice
3 green onions sliced - 1 small tomato diced
Mix with a fork and chill. Serve with tortilla chips

De Pere

Snicker Salad

8 oz thawed cool whip lite
1 pkg (4 1/2 oz serving) sugar free, fat free,
instant banana cream pudding
5-6 granny smith apples
6 large Snicker candy bars

Wash and core and cut apples into chunks.
Cut candy bars into small pieces
Fold pudding (dry) into cool whip.
Fold apples and candy pieces into cool whip mixture.
Enjoy!
Janeen Olson, De Pere

Front: Paula Battermann
Back: Janeen Olson, Jolene Zimmer, Dorene Batternamm

This is Edition #6 of the Tailgaten Cookbook Order Several For Gifts!

Tailgaten Cookbook   6th Edition   39

Creamy Potato Salad

1/2 cup milk
1 egg
1/3 cup sugar
4 tbsp butter
1/4 cup vinagar
1 1/2 tbsp cornstarch
3/4 tsp celery seed
3/4 tsp salt
1/4 tsp mustard

Cook ingredients, stirring constantly until thick and bubbly. While hot add 1/4 cup onion. When cool add 1/4 cup mayo and 3 hard cooked eggs. Mix with 7 large potatoes.

Sandee Evans, Sturgeon Bay

Sturgeon Bay

Tom Jorns, Sandee Evans, Cynthia Klapatch, Dale Klapatch

Green Bay

Pam "Marty" Aerts and two fans

Need More Information About The Tailgaten Cookbook? E-mail Us At dsabatke@nconnect.net

Everyone Loves To Tailgate!

Manitowoc

Left to Right: Steve Pleuss, Chad Haupt, Paul Roekle, Sharie Roekle, Linda Haupt, Jerry Haupt

Broccoli & Cauliflower Salad

1 fresh broccoli & cauliflower cut up
8 oz bacon, fried and diced - 8 oz cheddar cheese, cubed
1/2 onion chopped
Dressing: 2 tbsp vinegar - 1/2 cup sugar - 1 cup Miracle Whip
Mix together, chill and serve.

Linda Haupt, Manitowoc

West Allis

Brian, Rudy, Mark Fantl, Susan Fantl, Keith and Front: Jim

Steak Sandwich

Trim the fat from a beef tenderloin and cut into 1 1/2 inch hunks, cutting across the grain. Hammer until tender. Put in plastic bag, add teriyaki sauce and soak for 1 hour. Cook on a very hot grill 2 minutes on each side. Serve on bun with grilled onions and steak sauce.

Mark Fantl, West Allis

Menomonee Falls

Joe Lau, Mark Meyer, Mark Thielke, Jeff Monday, Tom Latus

"Thilks Traffic Treats"

This is a postgame snack while the traffic passes you by!
Prepare your grill with a sheet of aluminum foil. Place "Pizza Rolls" on the grill.
Flip after 5 minutes and they are ready in 10. By the time you finish, traffic is gone!

Mark Thielke, Menomonee Falls

Mark and Joe's Heavyweight Brownies

3/4 cup baking cocoa - 1/2 tsp baking soda
2/3 cup butter, melted and divided
1/2 cup boiling water - 2 cups sugar - 2 eggs
1 1/3 cups all purpose flour - 1 tsp vanilla extract - 1/4 tsp salt
2 cups of dark chocolate chunks

In a large bowl combine, cocoa and baking soda: Blend in 1/3 cup melted butter. Mix until creamy. Add boiling water, mixture will foam and thicken when stirred. Stir in eggs, one at a time, sugar, remaining butter and vanilla. Add flour and salt. Mix. Stir in chocolate chunks. Pour into a well greased 9 x 13 pan. Bake at 350 for 30-35 minutes or just until brownies pull away from the pan. Cool before cutting and dust with powdered sugar. These are thick & heavy brownies packed with chocolate. Since there is no frosting, they pack well and are easy to take to a game. Line a shoe box with foil and you're all set.

Mark Meyer, Slinger & Joe Lau, Menomonee Falls

Fond du lac

Ann Marie Schultz, Cory Schultz, James Carroll, James J. Carroll Sr., Steve Stuebing

Whitefish Bay

Mary Linde, Marilyn Linde, Bruce Linde, Megan Linde

Brookfield

Carol & Tom Sternig

Low Fat SouthWestern Sausage Dip

16 oz fat free cream cheese with garden vegetables
8 oz fat free Jimmy Dean's sausage
15 oz can black beans, drained
16 oz jar thick & chunky salsa
1/2 cup chopped red pepper
1/2 chopped green onion

Spread cream cheese into 8 inch serving plate. Cook sausage until browned. Cool. Combine sausage, black beans and salsa. Spoon over cream cheese. Place small circle of red peppers on top of this mixture in the center of the plate. Encircle the red peppers with the green onions. Keep refrigerated until ready to serve. Serve with tortilla chips.

Ann Marie Schiltz, Fond du Lac

Bacon & Tomato Cups

1 can (8 rolls) crescent rolls
8 slices bacon, fried crisp & drained
1 medium tomato, finely chopped
1/2 small onion, finely chopped
3/4 cup shredded swiss cheese
1/2 cup mayonaise
1 tsp dried basil

Remove rolls from package and separate, cut each roll into thirds. Using your fingers, press 1 piece of dough into bottom and up the sides of each cup of ungreased miniature muffin pan. In medium mixing bowl, combine remaining ingredients and mix well. Using tsp drop mix in each cup. Bake in preheated over at 375 for 5-10 minutes or until crust is brown.

Carol Sternig, Brookfield

Tailgaten Cookbook   6th Edition   43

Antigo

Hot Cheese Dip

1 lb Velvetta cheese
1 cup ripe olives chopped fine
1 can mushrooms chopped
1/2 cup cream (half & half)
2 cans crab meat

Cube cheese in sauce pan, add cream. Place on low to medium heat and keep stiring. When melted add other ingredients and mix well. Keep warm in chafing dish or something similar. Serve with party rye or crackers. Also excellent as a cold spread.

Carol Van Alstine, Antigo

Rod Van Alstine, Bonnie Kasseckert, Carol Van Alstine, Marge La Bode

Winona, MN

Green Bay Baked Beans

2 lbs great northern beans
6 tbsp ketchup
6 tbsp molasses - 6 tbsp brown sugar
1/2 lb bacon
2 tsp salt
1 tsp dry mustard

Bring beans to a boil, add above ingredients and bake about 3 hours until tender at 350.

Ron Gunderson, Trempealeau, WI

Leroy "Whitey" Gunderson & Ron Gunderson

Madison

Black Bean & Corn Salsa

16 oz black beans, cooked and drained
16 oz corn drained
1/4 cup green chopped onion
1/4 cup red chopped onion
1/3 cup lime juice
3 tbsp olive oil
1/2 tsp red chili pepper powder
1 tsp ground cumin
1/2 cup fresh tomatoes chopped
salt & pepper to taste

Combine everything except tomatoes. Cover and chill at least 2 hours. Stir in tomatoes just before serving. Serve with corn chips.

Mary Hoffmann, Oregon

Dave Seibel & Mary Hoffmann

Carmel Apple Dip

8 oz cream cheese
1/4 cup white sugar
3/4 cup brown sugar
Blend 3/4 cup dry roasted peanuts, mix together.
Serve on whole apples or cut apples in wedges and dip in mixture.
Bonnie Bohman, Sheboygan

Sheboygan

Rick Bohman, Bonnie Bohman, Rick Bohman Jr., Chad Shaw

Hartland

Left to right : Renee Kandler, Connie Reddy, B.J. Droegkamp, Steve Droegkamp, Tammy Griffin, Paul Griffin, Mickie Heier, Fudd Kilpatrick, Rick Kandler, Dan Reddy

1-2-3 Snack Meatballs

1 1/2 tsp Worcestershire
1 small can evaporated milk
1 pkg onion soup mix
1 lb ground beef
2 cup ketchup
1 cup brown sugar
1 tbsp Worcestershire sauce
Mix first 4 ingredients. Heat broiler 5 minutes. Roll mixture into 1 inch balls. Broil 10 to 12 minutes, 4 inches from broiler. Mix sauce & last 3 ingredients well and heat to hot.
Renee Kandler, Hartland

Cheese Squares

12 oz montery jack cheese, divided, 6 oz medium cheddar, small can chopped mild chilies, drained, 2 eggs, 2 tbsp evaporated milk and 1 1/2 tsp flour. Slice cheese in 1/3" slices. place in 9 x 9 pan greased with butter. Place single layer of montery jack cheese. Then a single layer of cheddar, sprinkle with drained chilies, then another layer of montery jack. Beat eggs, milk and flour and pour over top. Bake at 275 for one hour. Slice to serve on club crackers. Reheat on foil for 5 to 10 minutes on your grill at Lambeau.
B.J. Droegkamp, Hartland

Chili Taco Chip Dip

8 oz cream cheese
15 oz can Hormel chili
1 cup shredded cheddar
Soften cream cheese and spread on microwavable plate. Heat chili, pour over cream cheese and sprinkle cheese over top. Warm in Microwave and serve with chips.

Tailgaten Cookbook   6th Edition   45

Beloit

Easy Turkey Pot Pie

2 deep dish pie crusts
2 cans cream of chicken soup
2 cups turkey leftovers
2 - 8 oz pkgs cream cheese softened
1 cup peas - 1 cup corn
1 tbsp onion flakes
1 tbsp onion salt
Preheat oven to 350. Mix all ingredients and pour into pie crusts. Cook for 1 hour.
Randy Thorson, Beloit

Randy Thorson, Steve Mayfield, James Keller Jr., Jason Thorson

Fresh Bratwurst

Use fresh bratwurst made with ground chives added and par boil up to three minutes. Grill on a hot grill till golden brown.
Ress Rieck, Jefferson

Jefferson

Russ Rieck, Ray Sindsermann, Robert Teeter, Mark Teeter

Everyone Loves A Good Cookbook!
Enjoy The Tailgaten Cookbook

Order Another For A Friend

Milwaukee

Front: Gail Gondek, Adam Lynch. Back: Daniel Reynolds, Bob Lynch

Do You Know A Store That Would Like To Sell The Tailgaten Cookbook?

Have Them Contact Us At 920-262-1856

Berlin

Shirley A. Handrich, "Bill" Wilfred Handrich, Julie Handrich, Quinten Salzwedel, Steven Handrich

Tortilla Dip

1 lb hamburger
8 oz cream cheese block
1 can Hormel chili con carne with beans
1 tbsp onion diced fine
1 tsp chopped green pepper
1/2 tsp onion - 1/2 tsp garlic salt

Brown hamburger and season with onion, green pepper and garlic salt. drain meat, add cream cheese in small pieces and the chili con carne. Stir often on low until cheese is melted. Serve warm with tortilla chips.

Shirley Handrich, Berlin

Brodhead

Front row: Jeremy Crull, Heidi Crull, Jason Burtness. Back row left to right: Al Miller, Ellen Miller, Tom Naatz, John Favreau, Bill Nyman, Dave Johnson, Keith Favreau

Dessert Pizza
Serves 16

1 pkg refrigerated slice and bake sugar cookie dough softened
1 - 8 oz pkg cream cheese softened
1/2 cup brown sugar packed
1/4 cup creamy peanut butter
1/2 tsp vanilla extract
2 medium apples peeled, cored and sliced
1/4 cup caramel ice cream topping
1/2 cup peanuts chopped

Preheat oven to 350. Shape dough into a ball. Place dough in center of pizza pan and flatten slightly with palm of hand. Using lightly floured rolling pin, roll out dough to a 14 inch circle, about 1/4 inch thick. Bake 16-18 minutes or until light brown. Cool 10 minutes. Loosen cookie from pan and cool. Combine cream cheese, brown sugar, peanut butter and vanilla in bowl and mix. Spread mixture over top of cookie. Arrange apples over cream cheese mixture and sprinkle with cinnamon. Drizzle hot caramel over apples and sprinkle with peanuts.

Ellen Miller, Brodhead

Tailgate Taco Dip
Serves 6

1 - 8oz pkg cream cheese softened
1 pkg taco seasoning mix
2 tbsp salsa
onion chopped
tomato chopped- green bell pepper chopped
lettuce shredded or torn in small pieces
1 - 8oz bag cheddar cheese shredded fine
assorted vegetables
tortilla chips

Mix cream cheese, taco seasoning and salsa together. Spread in a flat covered dish. Have all your vegetables chopped or torn, ready to assemble at Lambeau. When you are in the parking lot, assemble your dip. Put lettuce on first, then onion, tomato and green pepper. Put your cheese on last. I use the finely shredded cheese because it does not fall off the tortilla chips as much. I also chop my vegetables small. By assembling the dip at Lambeau, the dip does not get soggy as fast.

Ellen Miller, Brodhead

Milwaukee

Shrimp Dip

1 cup Hellman's mayonnaise
1 cup fancy shredded cheddar cheese
1 can tiny shrimp
1 small onion grated
dash of garlic salt
dash of Lawry's seasoning salt
Mix all ingredients together. Good served with crackers and or fresh vegies. This makes a very small amount and therefore, I suggest at least doubling the recipe.
Chris Serdynski, Franklin

Dorothy Raiford, Russ Raiford, Chris Serdynski, Matt Serdynski

Hot Italian Beef

2 - 15 ox cans tomato sauce
2 large green peppers, cored, seeded and cut into 1/2 inch slices
12 fresh large mushrooms sliced
4 medium onions sliced and divided
2 tsp salt - 2 tsp pepper
2 tsp garlic powder
2 tbsp dried oregano
2 tsp dried basil
2 tbsp ground cumin
1/4 cup packed brown sugar
6 dashes Worcestershire sauce
1 rump or sirloin-tip beef roast 4-5 lb
Additional salt, pepper and garlic powder to taste
1 cup red burgundy wine
15 sliced kaiser rolls

Cedarburg

Orv Shine, Bill Zachow, Mark Priewe

Combine tomato sauce, green peppers, mushrooms and half of the sliced onions in a medium saucepan. Simmer vegetables until tender over low to medium heat. Add salt, pepper, garlic powder, oregano, basil, cumin, brown sugar and Worcestershire. Stir and continue simmering 10 minutes longer. Refrigerate, covered until needed. Place beef roast in roasting pan with cover, season to taste with salt, pepper and garlic powder. Cover with remaining sliced onions. Pour water to depth of 1 inch into roasting pan. Add enough burgundy to bring level of liquid to 1 1/2". Cover and roast at 350 about 2 hours. remove from liquid and chill overnight. Slice very thin and heat sauce. Add meat to sauce and heat through. Makes 15 sandwiches. **Bill Zachow, Cedarburg**

Tailgaten Cookbook   6th Edition   49

Stevens Point

Lori Greene, Mike Bugni, Tom Bugni, Wendy Bugni

Woodville

Edye Hilgendorf, Anne Steffen, Ryan Hilgendorf, Mark Hilgendorf, Marcia Hilgendorf

Cream Cheese Bars

Base:
2/3 cup soft butter
2/3 cup brown sugar
2 cup flour
1 cup chopped nuts

Filling:
2/3 cup sugar
2 eggs
4 tbsp milk
1 tsp vanilla
2-8 oz cream cheese

Base: Mix butter, sugar, flour and nuts to crumbly stage. Save 1 1/2 cup for topping. Pat remaining crumbs into a 9 x 13 pan. Bake at 350 for 15 min. Filling: Mix sugar, cream cheese and eggs until creamy. Add all ingredients and beat well and pour into crust. Top with rest of topping and bake at 350 for 25 minutes. Cool and cut.

Marcia Hilgendorf, Woodville

Kenosha

Joe Malzahn, Diana Van Daalwyk, GiGi Rotonda, Chris Van Daalwyk, Ben Harbach

Hartland

Front row: Mary Bawiec, Tony Bawiec. Back Row: Mike Eggers, Lisa, Mike Memmel, Sharon Memmel, Mitch Elert, Bob Reshel

Spicy Turkey Chili is best if prepared the day before and simmered for several hours. Reheat on Coleman burner at Packer game.

Frozen Tundra Brownies

Cream 1/2 cup shortening
3/4 cup sugar
1/2 tsp vanilla
Add 2 eggs, one at a time, beating well after each.
Sift 3/4 cup flour
1/4 tsp baking powder
1/4 tbsp cocoa
Combine mixtures. Add 1/2 cup chopped nuts. Put in greased 12 x 8 pan and bake 25 minutes at 350. Cut 16 marshmellows in half. Add on top of brownies and bake 3 minutes.

Frosting
1/2 cup brown sugar
1/4 cup water
2 squares unsweetened chocolate and bring to a boil. Cook 3 minutes. Add 3 tbsp butter and 1 tsp vanilla. Cool, then add about 1 1/2 cup powdered sugar and thin with milk if needed. Spread over marshmellows.

Diane Van Daalwyk, Kenosha

Spicy Turkey Chili

Serves 12+
7 lbs ground turkey
5-10 cloves garlic minced
6 stalks celery diced
2 large onions chopped
6-7 tbsp chili powder to taste
salt and pepper to taste
Brown ingredients together.
add to above
1 bottle spicy bloody mary mix
1 large can stewed tomatoes
2-14 oz cans each of
Black beans, drain & rinse
Pinto beans, drain & rinse
Bush's medium chili beans
1 small jar medium chunky salsa
2 large cans tomato juice.
Top with shredded cheddar, raw onion, oyster crackers and hot sauce.

Sharon Memmel, Hartland

Tailgaten Cookbook   6th Edition   51

New Berlin

Mark Scheuber, Jennifer Scheuber, Jen Vogel, John Vogel

Chocolate Chip Cheesecake Ball

1 - 8 oz pkg cream cheese softened
1/2 cup butter softened
1/4 tsp vanilla extract
3/4 cup confectioner's sugar
2 tbsp brown sugar
3/4 cup miniature chocolate chips
3/4 cup finely chopped pecans
Graham crackers

In mixing bowl, beat the cream cheese, butter and vanilla until fluffy. Gradually add sugars and beat just until combined. Stir in chocolate chips. Form into a ball and roll in chopped pecans. Chill for at least 2 hours. Serve on graham crackers.

Jennifer Scheuber, Shorewood

Butler

Pulled Beef

3-4 lbs boneless chuck roast
1 tbsp Worchestershire sauce
1 pkg Lipton dry onion soup mix
garlic powder to taste
1 cup water

Trim fat from roast, place in slow cooker, sprinkle Worchestershire sauce, onion soup and garlic powder over the top. Flip roast over and back to original side coating both sides with seasonings. Add water and cook on high 6 to 8 hours. With a couple of forks, pull meat apart as soon it's tender and continue until all the meat is shredded.

Nancy Bielawa, Butler

Nancy Bielawa, John Visser, Jim Bielawa, Vern Visser

Carmel Crunchy Snack Mix

3 cup Rice Chex - 3 cups Cocoa Puffs - 2 cups frosted pretzels - 1 cup peanuts
Combine the above ingredients in a 9 x 13 pan and set aside
Glaze: 1/2 cup butter - 1 cup brown sugar - 1/4 cup lite Karo syrup
Bring to a boil and boil 4 minutes. Do not boil over.
Remove from heat and add 1/4 tsp cream of tartar, 1/4 tsp baking soda and 1/2 tsp vanilla. Pour over mix in baking pan and bake at 300 for 15 minutes, stir, then continue for 15 minutes.
Transfer to cookie sheet to cool. **Vera Visser, Whitefish Bay**

Park Ridge, IL

Steve Carlson, Jim Stoddard, Chris David

Onalaska

Mary Mueller, Bonnie McCann, Tom Jones, Sally McCann, John McCann

John's Brats
Charcoal 15-20 brats till done. Put brats in kettle with 20 oz jar of Open Pit barbacue sauce. Must be original (other flavors won't work). Add 20 oz of beer, any kind. Simmer for 1/2 hour or more, the longer it simmers the better the taste.
John McCann, Onalaska

Jacks Hot Big Apple
In a large pot, add 1 quart apple cider, 1 cup orange juice, 1 lemon sliced, 1 stick cinnamon and 1 tbsp whole cloves. Simmer about 10 minutes and then stir in 2 cups of gentleman Jack.
Serve in mugs.
Makes about 12 servings.
Jim Stoddard, Park Ridge, Il

Brookfield

Richard Kalal, Sharon Kalal, James Weber

Paul Horning Beef Stew
2 lb stew meat - 1 can tomato juice
3 tbsp tapioca
1 tbsp Worchestshire sauce
3 tbsp beef bouillon granules
1 tsp sugar - 1 tsp salt - 1/4 tsp pepper
1 qt. tomatoes with juice
2 cups diced potatoes - 1 cup chopped celery
2 cups sliced carrots - 1 chopped onion
Mix all ingredients and
bake covered for 5 hours at 250.
Bake this dish ahead and reheat on the grill. Its great!
Sharon Kalal, Brookfield

Tailgaten Cookbook   6th Edition   53

Green Bay

Hot Taco Dip

1 1/2 lbs hamburger
taco seasoning - salsa sauce
picante sauce
Mexican shredded cheese
Fry hamburger, add taco seasoning. Layer in Pyrex dish-hamburger, salsa, picante sauce and Mexican cheese. Heat in oven until cheese melts through. Stir and serve. If you wish you may add onions and peppers.
William Gozowski, Green Bay

Front: Mike Sanders. Left to right: Steve Girard, Don Haanen, Dave Henguinet, William Gorswski, Terry Krause, Mark Thurston, Kevin Nooyen

Menomonee Falls

Pineapple Angel Cake

1 box angel food cake mix
1 - 20 oz can crushed pineapple in own juices
Put both in mixing bowl and mix. Pour into grease free 9 x 13 pan. Bake at 350 for 35-40 minutes. Cut into 15 squares and serve with cool whip.
Gladys Schaubach, Menomonee Falls

Dennis Szalewski, Pete Schaubach, Gladys Schaubach, Peter Molzen, Paul Szalewski

The 6th edition of the Tailtgaten Cookbook $14.00

Elkhorn

Gene Lininger, Mike O'Donell, Chuck Werri, Rocky Schmidt

Calico Bean Bake

48 oz jar cooked great northern beans
dash of salt
1 can red kidney beans
1 large can butter beans
1 1/2 cups brown sugar

1 can green beans
1/4 lb cut-up bacon uncooked
14 oz bottle ketchup
3 tbsp prepared mustard
1/4 large onion chopped

Combine all ingredients, mix gently and place in bean pot, casserole dish or slow cooker. Bake at 300 uncovered for 5 to 6 hours, covering for the last hour. In slow cooker, this dish can be cooked on low overnight.

Mike O'Donell, Elkhorn

Burlington

Left to right:
Tom Darnieder
Cail Darnieder
Brandyn Hen
Jessa Roth

Tailgaten Cookbook   6th Edition

55

Puffed Walleye

2 lbs walleye fillets
(catfish works well too!)
1/3 cup finely crushed cheese-flavored crackers or chips
1 tsp parsley flakes
1/4 cup creamy dressing
(ranch and bleu cheese are very tasty)

Heat coals to medium heat. Mix crackers and parsley, set aside. Place 2 sheets of foil on top of each other. Spray foil with non stick cooking spray.

Brush both sides of fish with dressing, coat one side of fish with cracker mixture. Place fish, cracker side up on prepared foil. Place another sheet of foil on top and seal so that air cannot escape. Cook on grill for 20-25 minutes. The top sheet will rise and steam the fish.

Eden LaFond, Middleton

Middleton

Mark Nowacki and Eden LaFond

Burlington

Karen Christensen, Vern Christensen, Ed Roucka, Toni Roucka

Carmel Brownies

Melt 1 bag of Kraft caramels in 1/2 cup evaporated milk. Mix 1 box German chocolate cake mix, 3/4 cup melted butter, 1/3 cup evaporated milk and 1 cup chopped pecans. Press 1/2 dough into greased 13 x 9 pan. Bake at 350 for 6 to 8 minutes. While warm, sprinkle 1 cup chocolate chips over layer. Spread carmel mix over chocolate pieces then crumble remaining dough over caramel. Bake 18-20 minutes.
Cool and chill to set.

Toni Roucka, Burlington

Watertown

Front row: Paul Bleske, Stephanie Bleske, Susan Tesch, Jenny Saniter, Michael Crawford, Patrick Bleske, Connie Bleske. Back row, left to right: Mike Saniter, Toby Tesen, Don Nass, Chris Herman, Bob Nass, Jeff Cieslak, Dave Pendley

Best Beer Tailgaten Brats

Pre-cooked Sheboygan brats, Budweiser beer, onions & a stick of butter. Brown brats, soak in beer mixture for 1 hour minimum at medium heat.....

Patrick Bleske, Watertown

Want To Be In Next Years Tailgaten Cookbook?

E-mail us at dsabatke@nconnect.net
or call at 920-262-1856

Tailgaten Cookbook   6th Edition   57

Whitewater

Wayne Saxe, Edith Saxe, Scott Saxe, Kandie Saxe

West Allis

Dexter Lichtenstein, Shirley Lichtenstein

Our Menu At Lambeau

T-Bone Steaks with mushrooms and onions. Asparagus with cheese and mild peppers on top.
Quartered potatoes covered with chopped onions and green peppers.
Pickled mixed vegies and plenty of cold beers.

Mishawaka, IN

Seated: John Schultz & Dave Kunert. Standing left to right: Ray Rangel, Bruce Schultz, Debbie Schultz, Mary Rangel, Linda Kunert, April Schultz

Sub Sandwich Sauce

2 tbsp finely chopped onions
2 tbsp red wine vinegar
1 tbsp finely chopped fresh parsley
1 tsp finely chopped lush basil
2 tbsp olive oil
2 garlic cloves crushed

Mix all ingredients well, refrigerate 1 hour to blend flavors. Spread on your favorite sub sandwich.

Menasha

Standing: Jeanne McFarlane, Dave McFarlane,
Seated: Debbie Rowe, Dick Rowe

Death by Chocolate

Brownie mix
1/4 to 1/2 cup Kaluaha or any coffee liquor
instant chocolate pudding
3 Heath bars crushed
whipped topping

Bake brownie mix according to directions. After baked, put holes in it with a fork. Pour Kaluaha over the top, let cool. Break up brownies in little pieces, this will be the 1st layer. Mix instant pudding according to the directions. This will be the 2nd layer. Whipped cream is the 3rd layer. Repeat these layers ending with a few candy bar sprinkles for the top.

Jeanne McFarlane, Menasha

Tailgaten Cookbook   6th Edition

Fennimore

Dona's Taco Dip

1 pkg fiesta ranch dip mix
1 - 16 oz container sour cream
1/2 can of black olives
8 oz shredded cheddar cheese
Can add green onions, tomatoes or lettuce if you wish.
Mix all together and serve with Tostitos.
Great Tailgate Treat
Dona Engel, Fennimore

Darcy Slack, Bob Andrews, Char Andrews, Tim Slack, Dona Engel, Scott Engel

Milwaukee

Mike Linsenmeyer, Gene Dropp, Mary Dropp, Ed Dropp

Montreal Peppered Steak

1/2 cup vegetable oil - 1/4 cup soy sauce
4 tsp McCormick's grill mate - steak seasoning
1-2 lbs sirloin or strip steak

Mary Dropp, Milwaukee

Combine oil, soy sauce and steak seasoning in glass or rubbermain container with lid. Add steak and marinate 45 minutes to 1 hour per side. Transport to Lambeau Field, discard marinade and grill to desired doneness.

Burlington

Ellen Steinhoff, Bob Steinhoff, Todd Steinhoff, Kelly Renz Schmidt

Bloody Mary Mix

6 quarts of fresh tomatoes cored and quartered
1 cup each of onion, celery and carrots (use food processor)
3 garlic buds
3-6 jalepeno peppers
Simmer for 2 hours. Run through a food mill, save some of the pulp and discard the skins. Add 1 tsp canning salt for each quart. Place in quart jars and cook in water bath for 20 minutes with lids on.
Ellen Steinhoff, Burlington

Racine

Beef Fajitas

1 lb strip steak filleted thin and cut into strips
Goya lemon pepper seasoning
Garlic powder

Marinate steak with Goya and garlic powder for a least 30 minutes. Grill on hot grill and serve on warmed tortillas with lettuce, cheese, tomatoes and salsa.
Enjoy!
Julia Gonzales, Racine

Emily Gonzales, John Gonzales, Julia Gonzales

Brown Deer

Pat Ciocarelli, Ray Ciocarelli, Joan Schneider, Cecily Hamm, Sandy Hamm, Tom Levinson

Shrimp Mold

1 can cream of mushroom soup
1 envelope Knox gelatin mixed with 1/4 cup cold water
8 oz soft cream cheese
1 cup mayonnaise (must be mayo)
1/2 cup chopped green onions
1/2 cup chopped celery
1 can small shrimp

Heat undiluted soup and add gelatin.
Mix well and add soft cream cheese. Mix well.
Remove from heat and add rest of ingredients.
Refrigerate in mold. Serve with crackers.

Pat Ciocarelli, Brown Deer

Homemade Salsa

4 cups ripe tomatoes, cored and chopped
5 jalapeno peppers, seeded, cored and chopped
2 medium yellow onions, peeled and chopped
1/2 green bell pepper, cored, seeded and chopped
1 cup canned tomato sauce
1 tsp salt
1 tsp peeled and finely chopped or crushed garlic
2 tbsp chopped fresh cilantro
1 1/2 tbsp red wine vinegar
Salsa jalapeno to taste
Mix all ingredients and serve!
Theresa Reilly, Edgerton

Hanna's Guacomole

2 ripe avocados, peeled and mashed
juice of 1/2 lime
4 tbsp homemade salsa
pinch of ground cumin
1/2 tsp salt
1/4 tsp freshly ground black pepper
2 scallions, chopped
1 tbsp chopped fresh cilantro
Place all ingredients in a bowl and mash until chunky. Do not let the guacamole get too smooth. This recipe doesn't make much guacamole, so make double or triple the recipe.
Theresa Reilly, Edgerton

Edgerton

Front row: Karen Fox, Sue Fox, Rose Fox, LeAnn.
Back Row: Annette Fox, Teresa Reilly

Tailgaten Cookbook   6th Edition

Green Bay

Chris Pierquet, Tina Pierquet, Tami Pieschek, Kevin Pieschek

Sugar Cookies

1 cup sugar - 1 cup butter
1 cup powdered sugar - 1 cup Mazola oil
2 eggs - 1 tbsp vanilla
4 cups flour - 1 tsp salt
1 tsp cream tarter -1 tsp baking soda
Cream sugar and butter. Add powdered sugar and oil. Add unbeaten eggs and vanilla. Add salt, cream of tarter and baking soda. Blend in flour gradually. Chill mix for several hours. Make into small balls. Dip in sugar and flatten slightly with fork. Bake at 375 for 10-12 minutes. Guaranteed to melt in your mouth. Yield 4-5 dozen.

Tina Pierquet, Green Bay

Chicken Garden Medley

1 lb boneless chicken breasts - 1 garlic clove minced - 1/4 cup butter - 1 small yellow squash julienne
1/2 cup each of julienne green and sweet red pepper - 1/4 cup thinly sliced onion
2 tbsp flour - 1/2 tsp salt - 1/4 tsp pepper - 3/4 cup chicken broth - 1/2 cup half and half cream
8 oz angel hair pasta, cooked and drained
2 tbsp shredded parmesan cheese

Grill chicken breasts, cut into strips. Saute vegetables in 2 tbsp butter. Cook until crisp and tender. In a small saucepan, melt remaining butter. Add flour, salt and pepper and stir to form a smooth paste. Gradually add broth stirring constantly. Bring to boil and cook for 2 minutes or until thickened. Stir in cream and heat through. Pour over chicken and vegetables. Stir until mixed. Place pasta in a greased 2 qt. baking dish. Pour chicken mixture over top. Sprinkle with parmeson cheese. Cover and bake at 350 for 20 minutes. Uncover and bake for 10 minutes longer. Yield 4-6 servings.

Tina Pierquet, Green Bay

There are copies of all 5 back editions of the Tailgaten Cookbook available. These are real collectors items. All different photos and recipes. See order form in back of book!

Neenah

Bob "Bugs" Weber & Shirlee Weber

The Best Ever Taco Dip

Step #1
2 pkgs cream cheese softened
1 1/2 pkg taco seasoning
1/4 cup sour cream
Beat above 3 ingredients and spread in a large round pizza pan and chill

Step #2
1 lb hamburger browned
1 can Bushes chili hot beans
Do not drain beans
1 can Rotell diced tomatoes with green chilies. It comes in hot or mild
1 can Tostitos salsa, mild, medium or hot
1/2 pkg taco seasoning
Brown hamburger, add the rest of the ingredients and simmer for about 5 minutes. Chill and cool and spread on top of cream cheese mixture.

Step #3
4 cups finely shredded cheddar cheese
1 head chopped lettuce
2 large diced tomatoes
1 small can sliced black olives
1 cup sour cream
1/2 tsp sugar
1 cup bottled Ortega taco sauce
Sprinkle cheese on top of meat and beans mixture. Then add lettuce, tomatoes, and black olives. Mix sugar with sour cream and drizzle in a ring on top of everything. Also drizzle taco sauce in a ring around top of dip.

2 Large bags taco chips. The big sturdy ones are the best.

Optional
Serve with 1 1/2 cup homemade guacamole, spooned only in center of dip, on top of everything.

Steps 1 & 2 can be done 1 day ahead. Once you have done step 3, you should serve within 2-3 hours.

Shirlee Weber, Neenah

It may take a while to make, but it is well worth it!

Beloit

Harry Zimmerman, Laurie Zimmerman, Sandy Valdez, Joe Valdez

Joe's Barbeque Sauce

Anybody can open a jar of bar-b-que sauce and slap it on our ribs or chicken; but if you like to spice it up and give it a little kick try this:

A bottle of your favorite sauce. I suggest Sweet Baby Ray's.
Bell Peppers, onions, tomatoes sliced Put with your sauce in a good size pan. Dash of garlic, salt, cumin, black pepper and seasoning salt. Add A-1, liquid smoke, ketchup, spicy mustard and some tabasco!
Boil till veggies are tender and apply to your favorite meats to grill and enjoy!

Joe Valdez, Beloit

Appleton

Bob Turek, Doreen McHugh, Tim McHugh, Rich Kowalski, Marsh Kowalski, Gary Ludwig

De Pere

Beer Dip

16 oz cream cheese
1 pkg Hidden Valley
ranch dip mix
1/2 cup beer

Mix and sprinkle finely shredded cheddar cheese on top

Use any kind of cracker to dip. Keep an eye on this dip because it will become a real favorite at Lambeau if the secret gets out!
Ann Leasum, De Pere

Ann Leasum, Sandy Janssen, Jill DePrey

Stevens Point

Crab Pizza Spread

12 oz cream cheese
1 tbsp Worchestershire sauce
1 tbsp lemon juice
few drops hot sauce
2 tbsp mayonnaise
small grated onion
Spread mixture (rounded) on plate. Top with 1/2 bottle chile sauce, 1 can crab meat and fresh parsley. Serve with Ritz crackers.
**Gerry Hudson,
Stevens Point**

Dave Galecke, Gerry Hudson, Scott Schweinfurth, Wayne Schweinfurth

Tailgaten Cookbook   6th Edition

Green Bay

Cream of Shrimp Soup Dip

1 pkg 8 oz cream cheese
1 can cream of shrimp soup
1 tsp lemon juice
garlic salt
paperka
1 can tiny shrimp

Mix all ingredients in blender exept for tiny shrimp. Fold in tiny shrimp.
Janice Anderson, Green Bay

Sue Draeger, Larry Draeger, Janice Anderson, Bob Anderson, Wayne Vande Hei, Rhea Vande Hei

The Tailgaten Cookbook 6th Edition Get One For A Friend!

Wausau

Spiced Nuts

1 tbsp water
1 slightly beaten egg white
1 cup dry roasted peanuts
1/2 cup unblanched whole almonds
3/4 cup sugar
1 tbsp pumpkin pie spice
3/4 tbsp salt

Conbine egg and water. Add nuts. Toss in large bowl. Add sugar, spice and salt. Place in a single layer on a greased cookie sheet. Bake at 300 for 30 minutes. Cool on waxed paper. Break into clusters.
Libby Mosher, Elcho

Clair Jowett, Colleen Jowett, Libby Mosher, Gene Mosher

Green Bay

Joe Falish, Bob Schumacher, Brad Schumacher

Algoma

Bill Ouradnik, Alger "Oldie" Olson II, Amanda Vanden Avond, Bernie Vanden Avond

Grilled Alaskan Scallops

Thaw and drain scallops, pat dry with a paper towel. Wrap each scallop with one strip of bacon. Pierce with toothpick to hold bacon in place. Place scallop wraps on grill, Done whenWhite-opec color.
Julie Handrich, Berlin

Red Salmon Spread

6 oz smoked red salmon flaked
12 oz cream cheese
2 tbsp sour cream
let cream cheese stand at room temperature for about 1 hour. Combine all ingredients. Serve in crackers, or bagel chips.
Julie Handrich, Berlin
(see tailgaten photo on page 46)

**Do You Know
A Retail Business
That Would Like
To Sell The
Tailgaten Cookbook?**

**Have Them Call Our
Home Office At
920-262-1856**

Tailgaten Cookbook   6th Edition   69

Green Bay

Mark Conrardy, Kelly Conrardy, Ann Vorpahl, Tom Vorpahl

Sobieski

Front row, Trisha Frank, Denise Brefczynski.
Back row, Pam Nicklas, Lois Drath

Paul Horning Stew

Bite Size Pieces
2 lbs beef stew meat
5 potatoes
6 carrots
1 cup celery
1 can tomatoes
1 small can peas drained
1 slice bread cubed
2 onions
4 tbsp tapioca
1 tbsp sugar
Mix all together and bake 5 hours at 250.
This is an old recipe.
Lois Drath, Sobieski

Tailgaten Cookbook 6th Edition

Seymour

Beer Dip

2 pkgs cream cheese
1 pkg Hidden Valley Ranch dry dressing mix
1/2 can beer
2 cups shredded cheddar cheese
Mix cream cheese, dressing mix and beer until smooth. Add 1 cup cheese and mix together. Top with remaining cheese. Serve with pretzels.
Kim Marnocha, Seymour

Front row, Joshua Marnocha, Second row, Kim Marnocha, LaRae Gracyalny, Back Row, Joe Kuhar, Greg Marnocha, Sherry Berndt, Dave Gracyalny

Appleton

Ham & Cheese Sandwiches

1/2 cup butter
1/4 cup minced onion
2 tbsp poppy seeds
1/4 cup prepared mustard
1/8 tsp accent
Mix together and spread on top and bottom halves of buns. Add a slice of ham and a slice of swiss cheese to each bottom half. Cover with top half. Wrap in foil. Bake at 350 for 20 minutes and serve warm.
Dick A. Novitske, Appleton

Jim Schultz, E. J. Novitske, David L. Novitske, Richard A. Novitske

Tailgaten Cookbook   6th Edition   71

Fond du Lac

Snicker Salad

2 sticks margarine
2 cups powdered sugar
1 egg
20 oz crushed drained pineapple
11 oz cool whip
2 cups granny smith apples
4 to 6 snickers candy bars cut up
Mix together margarine, sugar, and egg with mixer. Add rest of ingredients.
Eat and enjoy!
Kris Hodorff, Fond du Lac

Dave Hodorff, Kris Hodorff, Margret Wilson, Jeff Wilson

Green Bay

Wendi Lemens, Brian Lemens, Steve Zeise, Carolyn Zeise, Bonnie Zeise, John R. Zeise

Chili Taco Chip Dip

Spread 1 large pkg. cream cheese in microwavable baking dish, 1 can Hormel chili, 1 jar salsa & top with grated cheddar cheese. Microwave until cheese is melted. Serve with taco chips.
Carolyn Zeise, Green Bay

Tailgaten Cookbook   6th Edition

Kaukauna

Front row: Harold Olson, Dutch DuChateau Back row, left to right: Jeff DuChateau, Jenny Schuh, Friend, Lyn DuChateau, Dan Pawlowski, Julie Vanderloop, Ceil DuChateau, Fay Olson

Some Of The Best Recipes On Tailgaten Are Found In The 6th Edition of the Tailgaten Cookbook!

Let A Friend In On The Secret...........
Buy Them A Copy Today

Tailgaten Cookbook   6th Edition   73

Green Bay

Crab & Shrimp Spread

16 oz cream cheese softened
small bottle Hoffman House
shrimp sauce
4 cans white crab meat
3 cans small broken shrimp
(both well drained)
Salt & pepper
lemon juice optional

Combine cream cheese and shrimp sauce until smooth, fold in crab and shrimp and season with salt and pepper. Add approx. 1/2 tsp lemon juice and chill for 2 hours

Kim Amenson, Green Bay

Amanda Amenson, Kim Amenson

Appleton

Tom Gage, Laura Gage, Greg Croft, Mary Croft

Malted Milk Ball Brownies

1 pkg fudge brownie mix
1/2 cup water (1 1/2)
1/2 cup oil (1 1/2)
1 egg (2)
1/2 cup chopped malted milk balls 1 1/2

Frosting:
1 cup semi sweet chocolate chips
2 tbsp butter - 2 tbsp milk
1/4 tsp vanilla
1/3 cup coarsely crushed malted milk balls

BROWNIES: heat oven to 350. Grease bottom only of 13 x 9 pan. In large bowl, combine all ingredients. Bake 35 minutes. Do not overbake. Cool completely. FROSTING: In small saucepan over low heat, melt chocolate chips and butter, stirring constantly until smooth. Remove from heat. Add milk and vanilla, blend well. Spread frosting over cooled brownies. Sprinkle with crushed malted milk balls. Refrigerate 10-15 minutes. **Mary Croft, Appleton**

Minneapolis, MN

Mike Steffek, Kara Phillips, Jim Phillips

Neenah

Front row: Jace Fenton, Dick Bertruam. Second Row: Tom Fenton, Marcia Brodt, Lynn Bertram,
Back row: Clar Brodt, Jeff Sherwood, Alan Sherwood, Guy Miller

Tailgaten Cookbook   6th Edition

Appleton

Seated: Baylee Gordon, Second row: Bob Gordon, Pat McInnes, Nancy Hackinson, Donna Genda, Chris Genda, Dar Blahnik, Belinda Genda, Back row: John McInnes, Bob Hackinson, Jan Gordon, Scott Gordon, Steve Genda, Karl Blahnick, Judd Genda

Tailgate Beans

1/2 lb ground beef
1/2 lb bacon
1 medium onion, diced
2 large cans B & M beans
1 can (15 oz) kidney beans, drained
1 can (15 oz) butter beans, drained
1/2 cup brown sugar, packed
1 cup white sugar
3/4 cup ketchup
1/2 tbsp dry mustard
2 tbsp dark molasses

Brown bacon, drain. Brown ground beef, drain fat and add remaining ingredients. Bake 1 hour at 350 covered and 10 minutes longer uncovered. Best made one day in advance and reheated. Serves 8 to 10.

Pat McInnes, Appleton

Oshkosh

"Uncle Dan's" Famous Dip

Whisk together 2 pkg softened cream cheese with a 16 oz. jar of medium salsa. Mix in 2 1/2 tbsp Mrs. Dash original flavor seasoning. Sprinkle a little extra on top for garnish.
Serve with Tortilla chips.
Laurie Cross, Oshkosh

Laurie Cross, Tim Cross, Anita Pierce, Dee Pierce, Dan Cross, Diane Cross

Ringle

Brad Campbell, Paul Radtke, Steve Tarras, Tim Bob Fraser, Alan (Ziggy) Zieglmeier, Steve Tobalsky

Ziggy's Zesty Salsa

28 oz can crushed tomatoes
1 bunch green onions
1/2 small yellow onion
1 stalk celery (optional)
1/2 green pepper
7 jalepeno peppers
(More or less to taste)
4-5 cloves garlic
black pepper

Dice onions, including the greens, celery, green pepper and jalepeno peppers. Press garlic through garlic press or chop finely and add to crushed tomatoes. Add other diced ingredients. Can be refrigerated and eaten fresh or bring to a slight boil, pour into hot canning jars, seal with boiled lids and let cool. For a hotter flavor add 1 or 2 habenero peppers.
Ziggy Zieglmeier, Rothschild

Tailgaten Cookbook   6th Edition   77

Green Bay

Guacamole

2 large avacados, peeled and mashed
1 medium tomato
2 tbsp green onions
2 tbsp lemon juice
1/2 tbsp garlic salt
(or 2 cloves garlic)
1/2 tsp salt
Combine all ingredients in bowl and mix to consistency desired. Chill and serve with tortilla chips or use burritos, fajitas, tacos or sandwiches.
**Debra Meister
Green Bay**

Left to right: Gerald Meister, George Schmidt, Jimbo Schleis, Daniel Wellner, Debra Meister, Kim Destree, Robert Roth, Brenda Wellner, Gena Castro

Sobieski

Fizzy Fuzzy Navel

1/3 bottle peach schnapps
1 bottle champagne
2 cans Sierra Mist
or any white soda
16 oz orange juice
**Cindy DeQuaine
Sobieski**

Cindy DeQuaine, Peter Lemmer, Patti Stewart, Mathew Wirt

Beloit

Kevin Messman, John Malizio, Kurt Matschall, Steve Miller

Stevens Point

Liz Hoover-Greenwald, Sue Pierce, Judi Janquart

Cocktail Sausages

Small jar grape jelly
15.5 oz can regular or BBQ Manwich
Chili sauce (to taste)
Cocktail sausages (75-85)
In electric fry pan mix chili sauce, grape jelly and Manwich. Simmer. Add sausages and simmer.
Serve from crockpot
Judie Janquart, Stevens Point

Tailgaten Cookbook   6th Edition   79

Merrill

Beer Cheese Soup

1 qt water
4 chicken bouillion cubes
2 1/2 cups potatoes, cubed
1 cup celery, diced
1 lb California blend vegetables
2 cans cream of chicken soup
1 can beer
2 lbs Velveeta cheese, cubed

Boil together first 4 items for 10 minutes. Add remaining ingredients. Simmer until cheese is melted. If desired, serve with popped popcorn for garnish.

Crystal Krueger, Merrill

Crystal Krueger, Patricia Thieme

Green Bay

Front row: Pete Lukowitz, Ione Lukowitz, Arielle Carley, Francene Carley, Jan Lukowitz, Che Lukowitz, Tom Carley

Garlic Surprise Cannon Balls

1 lb. ground spicey pork sausage
1-16 oz pkg shredded cheddar cheese
50 fresh, peeled garlic cloves
1 to 2 jalepeno peppers
or 4 oz. can or jar diced
2 cups baking mix

Blanch 50 cloves of garlic in boiling water for 3 to 4 minutes. Drain and set aside to cool. Preheat oven to 350. In large bowl combine sausage, cheese and baking mix. Form mixture into 1 1/2 inch balls inserting a blanched garlic clove in each. Place balls on an ungreased baking sheet and bake 30 to 40 minutes or until golden brown. Serve hot. To bring to tailgate party use pyrex 9 x 12 inch pan with microwavaable insert and case for traveling. Depending on the size of the balls will make 48-50 servings.

Francene Carley, Green Bay

Kaukauna

Left to right: George "Porgie" Burton, Dan King, Scott Buchinger, Kathy Volz, Karen Wild, Lori Linzmeyer, Lisa Dercks, Larry Wild

Sioux Fall, SD

Melinda Huntimer, Leroy Huntimer, Derrick Miller, Jim Ellis

Green Bay

Jerry Anderson, Sue Anderson, Gail Kivi, Creg Kivi

Marinated Beef Brisket

1/4 cup liquid smoke
1/2 tsp garlic powder
1/2 tsp onion salt
1/2 tsp celery salt
4 to 6 lb fresh brisket
Barbecue sauce

Place brisket, fat side down in a glass pan. Sprinkle with smoke, garlic powder, onion salt and celery salt. Cover with foil and refrigerate overnight. When ready to bake, turn fat side up. Wrap and seal in foil. Bake at 275 for 1 hour per pound. Before last hour of baking time, pour off half the liquid and pour on barbecue sauce to cover meat. Cool before slicing thin. Seal again and reheat. Great on rolls for tailgating.

Sue Anderson, Ironwood, MI

Blueberry/Cherry Angel Food Dessert

16 oz angel food cake torn into pieces
3.4 oz. pkg instant vanilla pudding
1 cup sour cream
1 1/2 cup milk
1 can of blueberry or cherry pie filling.

Put half the torn pieces of angel food cake into an 8 x 11 1/2" glass dish. Combine instant vanilla pudding and milk. Mix until smooth and slightly thickened. Blend in sour cream. Spoon half the pudding mixture over the angel food pieces. Repeat layers. Smooth top with spatula. Spread blueberry or cherry pie filling on top.
Refrigerate several hours.

Gail Kivi, GreenBay

Lambeau Field Pack Rats

The Founders
Daniel "Dog" Henning, Oshkosh
Randy "Doob" Franklin
Anchorage AK

Yah der hey...adopt us today!

www.thepackrats.com

The Pack Rats
1st. & 2nd Editions

Introducing the Lambeau Field Pack Rats

An amazing discovery has been made in Green Bay, Wisconsin. The hidden world of a very shy but friendly mouse-like greature was discovered in the tradition filled Lambeau Field during its renovation. Scientists called in to investigate have named his sub-species pack-rrr-rattus adoptus.
(for the full story of this amazing discovery please visit the Pack rats website at: www.thepackrats.com)

Pack rats are available as numbered, limited editions of 60,890 (the pre-renovation capacity of Lambeau Field) The 1st. Edition "Curly" (Home Team Colors) and 2nd Edition "Curly" (Away Team Colors) can now be adopted at the Packer Pro Shop, thepackrats.com and adoption centers established at businesses near you. Personalized adoption certificates for each Pack Rat are available at thepackrats.com. $4.00 from each Pack Rat adoption and $1.00 from each adoption certificate purchased will be donated to the Packers for Lambeau Field capital improvements. To adopt a Pack Rat or for more information go to thepackrats.com or call

920-231-7250

Tailgaten Cookbook   6th Edition

Appleton

Front row: Jim Schmidt, Sandra Thein-Schmidt, Kathy Sager Ann Sager, Kaye Seidl, Ron Sager,
Back row: Earl Sager, Joe Seidl,

Meatballs in Beer Sauce

1 lb lean ground beef
2 cups soft bread crumbs
1/4 cup milk
1 egg beaten
3 tbsp finely chopped green pepper
3 tbsp finely chopped onion
1 tsp salt
3/4 tsp poultry seasoning
1/4 tsp pepper
1 tbsp veg. oil
1 - 12 oz beer at room temp.
1 cup catsup
2 tbsp Worchestershire sauce
1 tbsp sugar
1 tbsp cider vinegar

In a medium bowl, combine beef, bread crumbs, milk, egg, green pepper, onion, salt, poultry seasoning and pepper, mixing well.
Shape into 40 meatballs. In a 10" non stick skillet over medium high heat, brown meatballs, half at a time, in oil. Transfer to paper towels to drain.
In a dutch oven or 3 qt. sauce pan, stir beer, catsup, Worchestershire sauce, sugar and vinegar until blended over medium high heat. Bring to boil. Add meatballs, reduce heat to low, cover and simmer for 15 minutes. Uncover and simmer 15 minutes longer to slightly thicken the sauce.
Serve with picks.

Kathy Sager, Appleton

Great Gift Idea

Tailgaten Aprons

White Poly-cotton twill.
Wide binding.
Continuous tiestrings.

Close-out Special

$5.00

Plus $3.00 Postage, Handling, Sales Tax

Total Price **$8.00**

Yes, send me _____ Aprons at $8.00 each (A $17.77 value)

Name_____ Address_____

City_____ State_____ Zip_____

Make checks payable to and mail to: **Tailgaten Cookbook**
N8443 Swansea Drive
Ixonia, WI 53036

Tailgaten Cookbook   6th Edition

Tailgaten Cookbook Back Editions

Edition #1. 1996 Season
Our first Tailgaten Puablication. 90 Photographs of the fans, most taken during the cold weather. Some great recipes. Very few of this edition left. A real collectors item.

Edition #2. 1997 Season
The Green and Gold checkered board cover make this book stand out on any newstand. Over 100 group photo's of the fans and over 200 great recipes for tailgaten, all new and all great!

Edition #3. 1998 Season
The tailgater and his pick-up, a familar sight at lambeau, is on the cover of this great issue. This has been one of the most popular editions and has sold all over the world. A must for your Packer collection.

Edition #4. 1999 Season
The only Tailgaten edition with Snow on the cover. No matter how hot or how cold the weather is, the Packer tailgaters are doing their thing every home game at Lambeau.

Edition #5. 2000 Season
The biggest edition ever. Hundreds of "all NEW" Tailgaten Recipes and over 100 hundred photos of Tailgaten Groups.

Send me the following:
_____ Edition #1 _____ Edition #2 _____ Edition #3 _____ Edition #4 _____ Edition #5
Each book is $17.77 and includes postage, handling and sales tax of $.77.
Mail to: Name_____ Address_____
City_____ State_____ Zip_____
Send to: Tailgaten Cookbook, N8443 Swansea Dr., Ixonia, WI 53036

The Great Tailgaten Recipe Hunt!

We are starting to put together Edition #7 of the Tailgaten Cookbook and starting to gather recipes.

E-Mail Us Your Favorite Tailgaten Recipe

dsabatke@nconnect.net

Thank You

Disclaimer

With many cities represented in this 6th edition of the Tailgaten Cookbook, over 100 photos appear, representing several hundred tailgaters, plus their recipes. We gather all of our information including the names under the photos and the recipes from these people and dealing with this many people is bound to create mistakes just with handwriting alone. We make every effort to eliminate any mistakes and spend countless hours contacting people to make sure that we have everything right. Please excuse us if you find a mistake and enjoy the 6th edition of the Tailgaten Cookbook.

Thank You!

From all of us at the Tailgaten Cookbook

If you would like to contact us:
Tailgaten Cookbook
N8443 Swansea Drive
Ixonia, WI 53036
Phone 920-262-1856
Fax 920-262-2499
E-Mail dsabatke@nconnect.net

Tailgaten Cookbook 6th Edition Order Form

The NEW 6th Edition Tailgaten Cookbook is Just $14.00 each
Plus $3.00 Postage & Handling and .77 Sales Tax

Name_____

Address_____

City_____

State_____Zip_____

Please send _____ copies of the 6th Edition at $17.77 each
(Includes postage, handling and .77 cents sales tax)

Back Issues of The Tailgaten Cookbooks

Please send editions ____#1____#2____#3____#4____#5
Total cost per book is $17.77
(Includes postage, handling and .77 Sales Tax)
Great Collectors Items

Make checks payable to and mail to:
Tailgaten Cookbook
N8443 Swansea Drive
Ixonia, WI 53036